Does a Rabbit Lay Eggs?

by Mrs. Finocchiaro's and
Mrs. Klabunde's classes
with Tony Stead

capstone

All living things have a **life cycle.** Life starts at the beginning and goes around in a circle.

Some animals start out as **eggs.** Others start out very little and grow to be adults.

There are steps to becoming an adult. We have written about and illustrated different life cycles.

egg: a round or oval object in which young animals develop

life cycle: the series of changes that take place in a living thing, from birth to death

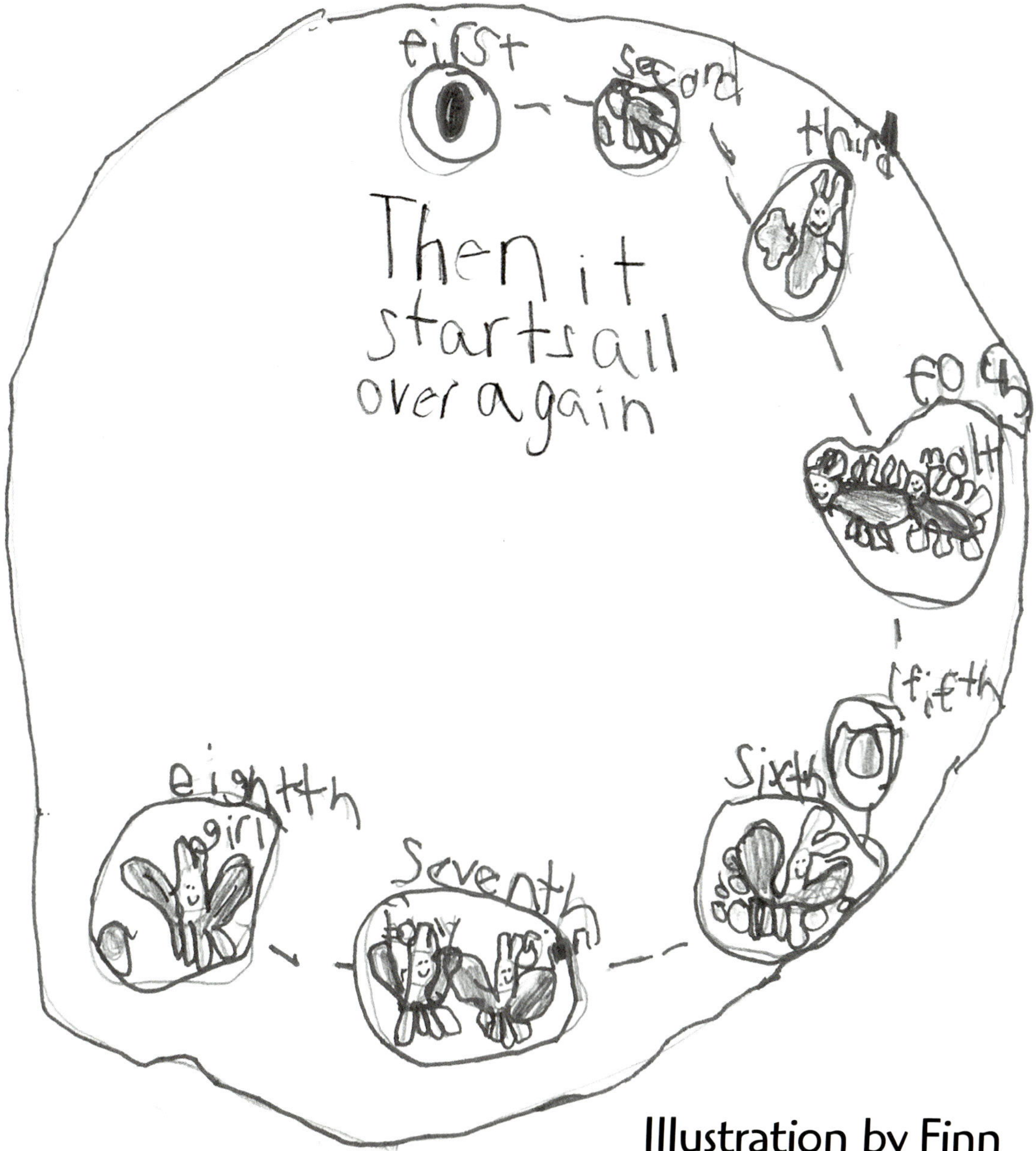

Illustration by Finn

The Life Cycle of a Fish

by Maya

A fish starts out as a tiny egg. After a few days, it **hatches** and starts swimming. It gets some skills.

It becomes an adult after a little while. It can lay eggs. Male fish **fertilize** the eggs, and the life cycle starts again.

fertilize: to cause an egg to develop a new animal

hatch: to break out of an egg

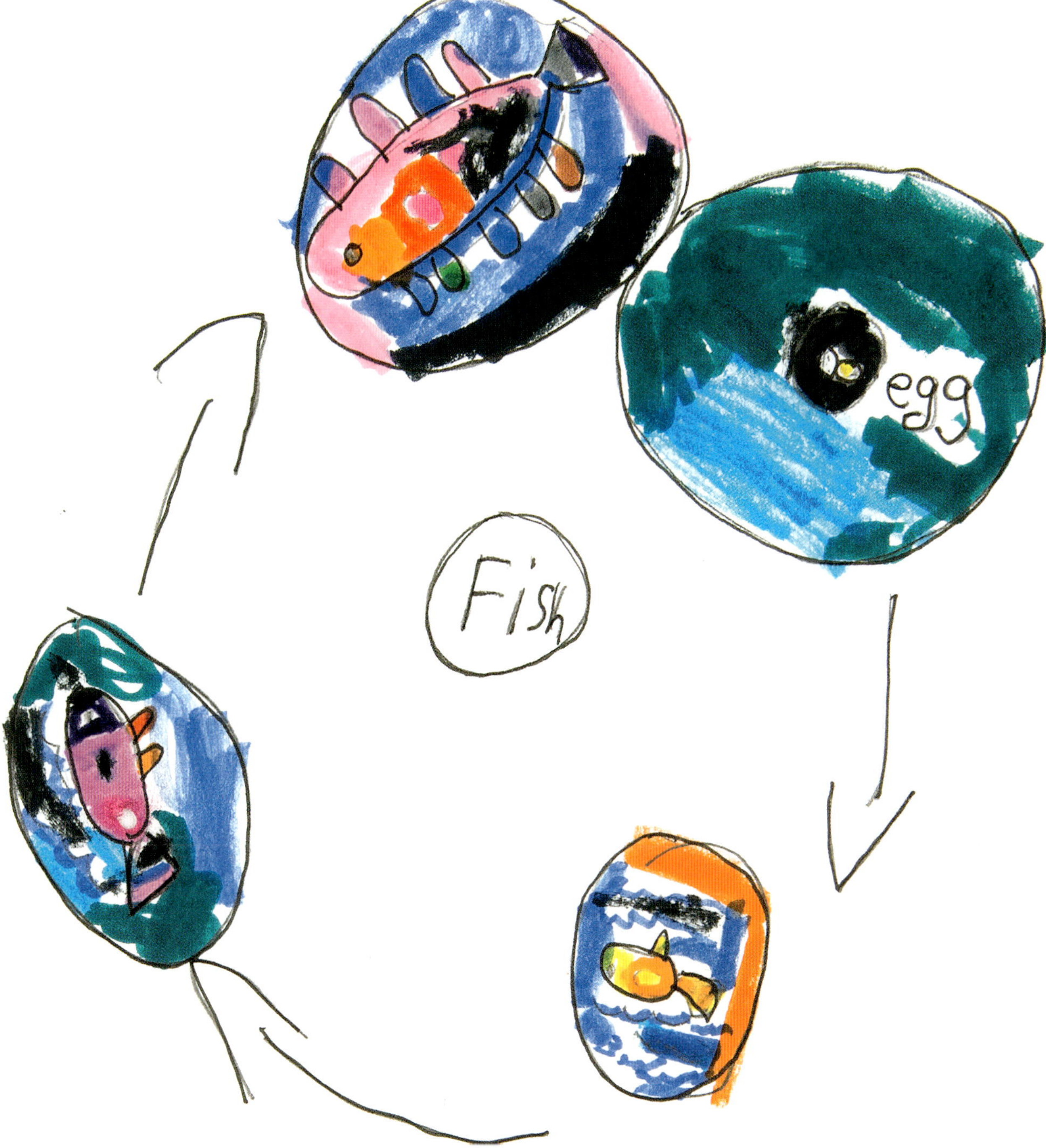
Fish
egg

The Life Cycle of a Bird

by Caleigh, Emily, and Peyton

A bird begins in an egg. Then it hatches and out comes a baby bird. The baby bird will eat worms from its parents.

Then it will grow feathers and will continue to grow and grow. After some time goes by, it's an adult. The bird can lay an egg.

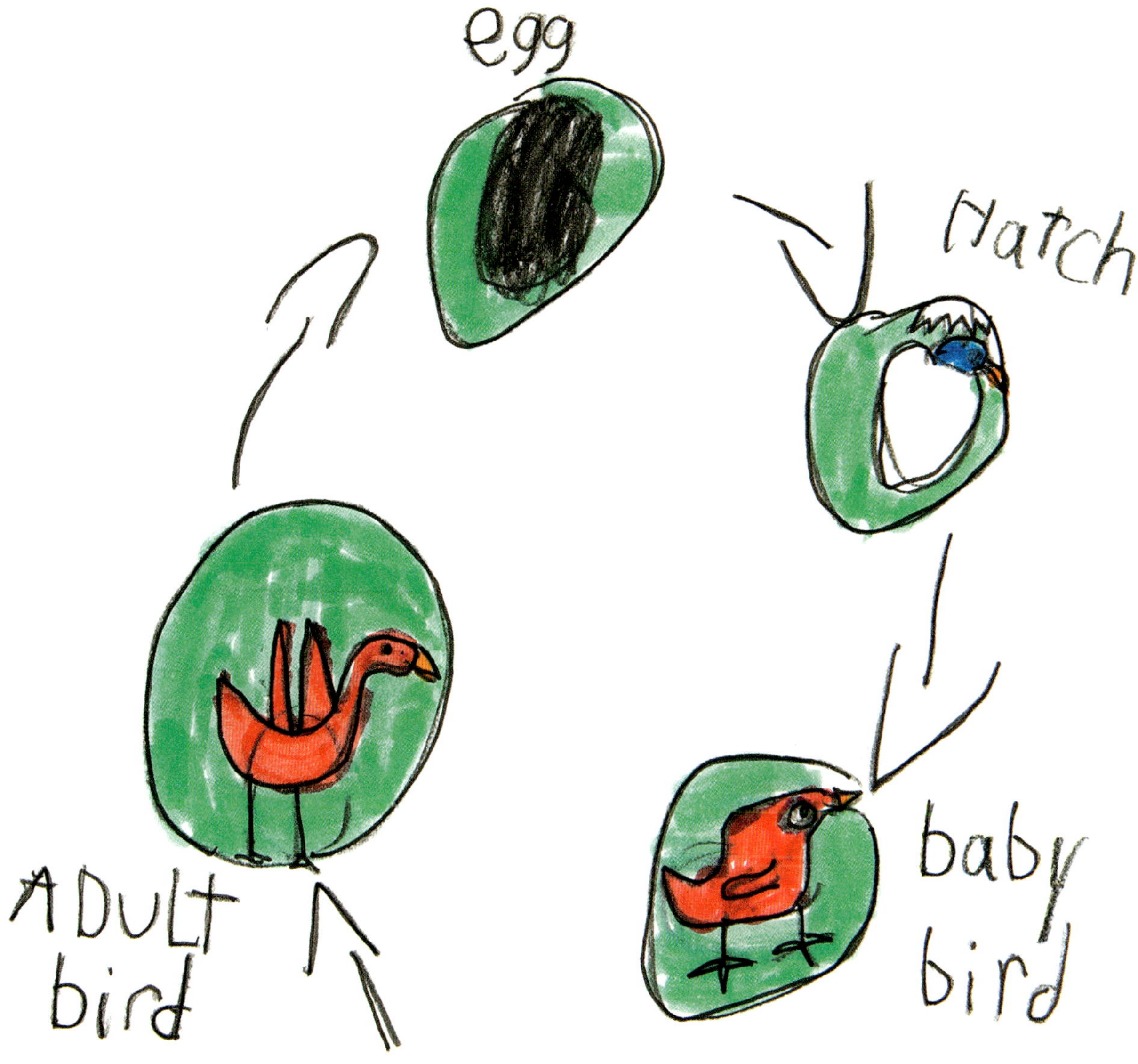
egg
Hatch
baby bird
ADULT bird

The Life Cycle of a Dragonfly

by Clayton

First, the baby insect comes out of an egg. Then, it becomes a **nymph**, or **larva.** It sheds its skin as it grows. This is called **molting.**

Then it comes above ground. It comes out of its skin. Finally, it becomes an adult dragonfly.

larva: an insect at the stage of development between an egg and an adult

molt: shedding fur, feathers, or an outer layer of skin; after molting a new covering grows

nymph: a young form of an insect; nymphs change into adults by shedding their skin many times

The Life Cycle of a Sea Turtle

by Atlee and Elisabeth

The life cycle starts when an adult sea turtle lays eggs. Next, the eggs hatch in the sand. Then, baby turtles come out of their eggs. After that, they move to the water, and they get bigger and bigger.

The sea turtles learn how to hunt fish or jellyfish. Last, they find a mate and the life cycle starts all over again.

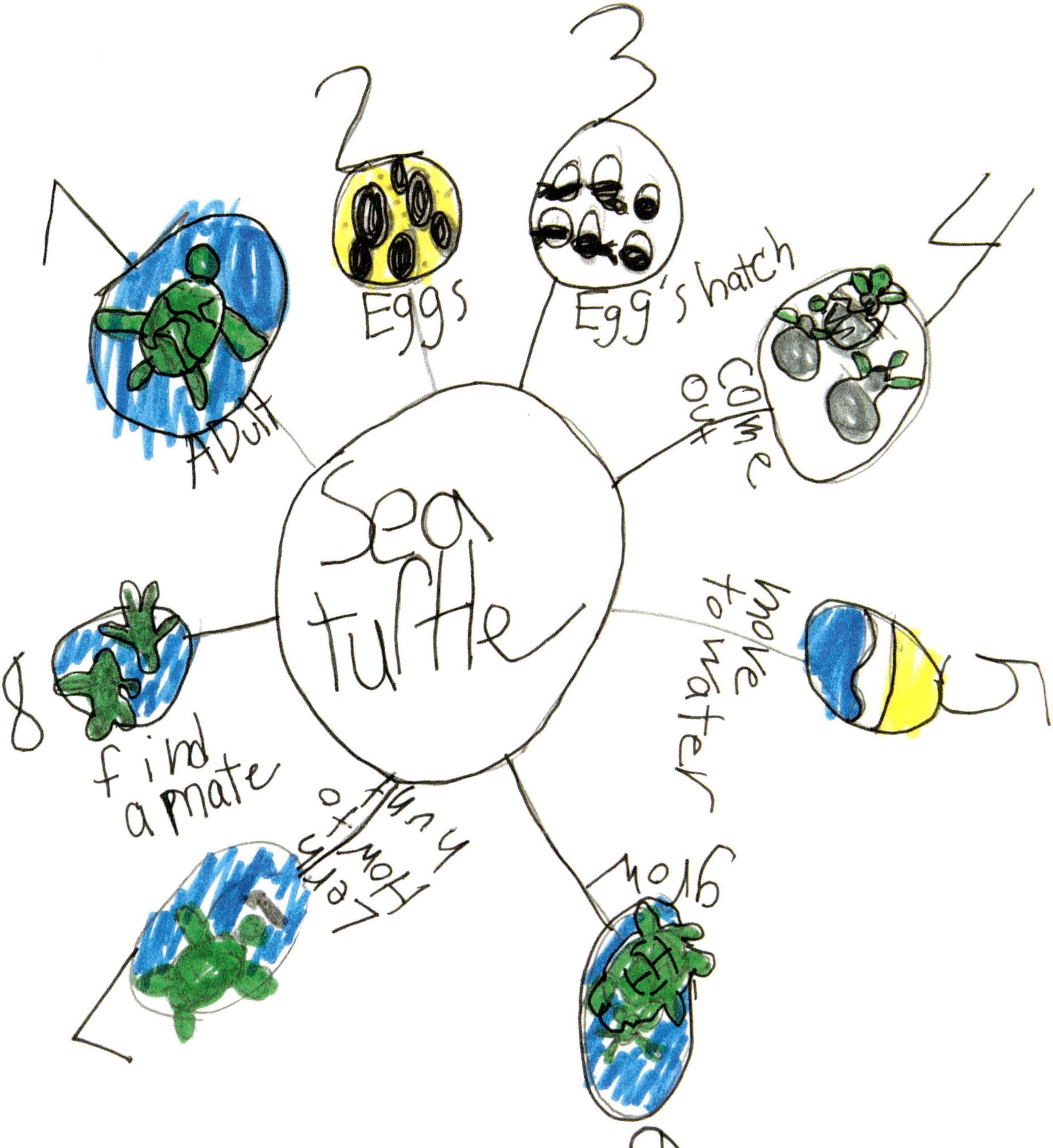
Sea turtle
1
Adult
2
Eggs
3
Egg's hatch
4
come out
5
move to water
6
grow
7
turn to home
8
find a mate

The Life Cycle of a Dolphin

by Erin

First, an adult dolphin has a baby. The baby dolphin looks like its parent, but it is smaller.

The little baby grows and grows. It learns how to hunt. Then, it's big and is an adult. The dolphin can start the life cycle all over again.

2.
3.

The Life Cycle of a Frog

by Gillian

The life cycle of a frog begins with thousands of eggs. Some mother frogs watch over the eggs.

Then, the eggs hatch. Tadpoles come out of the eggs. After six to nine weeks, the tadpoles grow their back legs. After 12 to 16 weeks, the tadpoles have turned into adults. Now that they are adults, they can start the life cycle again.

A life cycle is a **pattern** that goes on and on forever. The animal changes and grows bigger with each **stage**.

Now that you know a little more about life cycles, do you think a rabbit lays eggs?

pattern: an arrangement that is repeated in the same way several times

stage: a step in a process or development